How to Make jewelry from junk

How to

Make jewelry from junk

Sharon Finmark
and David Wickers

Studio Vista

Acknowledgments

The authors would like to thank Emma and Simon de Lotz and David Aldridge for modelling some of the jewelry in this book. The photograph on page 20 is reproduced by permission of the Hawaii Visitors Bureau.

Studio Vista a division of
Cassell & Collier Macmillan Publishers Limited,
35 Red Lion Square, London WC1R 4SG
Sydney, Auckland, Toronto, Johannesburg

An affiliate of the Macmillan Publishing Co. Inc.,
New York

First published in Great Britain 1975

Filmset and printed in Great Britain by
BAS Printers Limited, Wallop, Hampshire

ISBN 0 289 70512 6

Contents

Introduction

Many people like to look at those glittering displays of jewelry in shop windows. Not so many can afford to buy and wear them. But diamonds, pearls, emeralds and all the other rare and precious stones are not the only jewels around.

All over the world, and through many centuries, people have been making their own jewelry from much simpler materials that were a part of their everyday life. These have been made and worn not only to look pretty, but even as a form of money and also in magic ceremonies.

In your own surroundings – the house and garden, nearby countryside or the city office – there is a wealth of not-wanted junk or odds and ends that can be turned into a wide variety of jewelry. An old alarm clock, for example, can be easily transformed into a beautiful pendant, old chicken bones can become a tribal necklace, and so on through a whole range of exciting possibilities. And your own gems can look even better than the 'real' thing!

Berries, seeds, pips and stones

The countryside, garden and fruit bowl can each help supply the ingredients for a nature bead necklace. Try to collect some of the following:

rose hips; hawthorn haws; blueberries; holly berries; bay berries; rowan berries; sunflower, bean and pumpkin seeds; apple, orange, lemon and melon pips; plum, peach, apricot, cherry and date stones.

Take a book on trees and shrubs along with you on your collecting trip so that you can avoid the poisonous types. Ask your family and friends to help and give them a box or jar to put things in.

You need:
needle and thread (or fishing line)
borax, salt and some sand
varnish (clear nail varnish)
hammer and nail
a small piece of wood (from an old broom handle perhaps)
file
plasticine
glue
matchsticks and curtain rings

1 When you have gathered enough seeds you must first wash and dry them. The airing cupboard makes an ideal drying area, or you can just lay them out in the garden on a warm, sunny day.

Berries, however, may grow wrinkled and even turn mouldy. If you want to keep your berry necklace, you should dry the berries more thoroughly. Put them in a mixture of borax, salt and sand (about twice as much borax to sand). Leave them in the mixture for a few days.

2 To add a little lustre to your beads you can use varnish or hair spray. You could also dye them, to make a colourful melon seed necklace, for example.

3 Use a hammer and nail to make a hole in the larger fruit stones, or make a special tool for the job. Hammer a long thin nail through the short piece of wood (one that you can comfortably hold in your hand). File the pointed end to make it really sharp.

4 Place the stone in a large lump of plasticine (or a vice if you have one) to hold it still while you make the hole.

5 Hold the tool in your hand and twist the nail through the centre of the stone.

You will be able to make the holes in the smaller seeds, pips and berries with the needle and thread as you join them together.

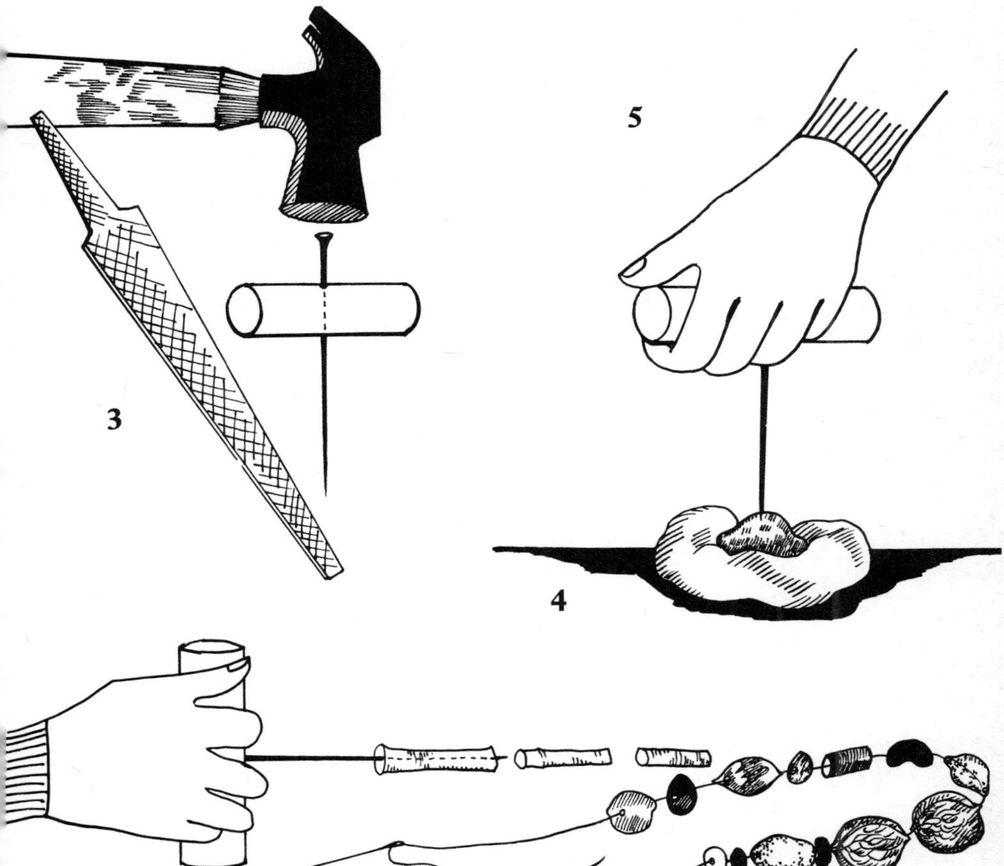

6 Sort out your jewels on the table. You may prefer to keep each type separate or mix them all together on the necklace. Some may look best hanging down from the thread, others lying flat.

7 When you have arranged the beads in order, tie a curtain ring to the end of the thread and add a blob of glue to the knot to stop the beads slipping off. Use a big needle and be sure to wear a thimble as you make the rest of the holes. Thread them all together.

8 When you think the necklace is long enough, tie the other end of the thread round a matchstick. Add a blob of glue to the knot to make it secure.

9 When the glue has dried, fasten the beads round your neck by putting the match through the ring.

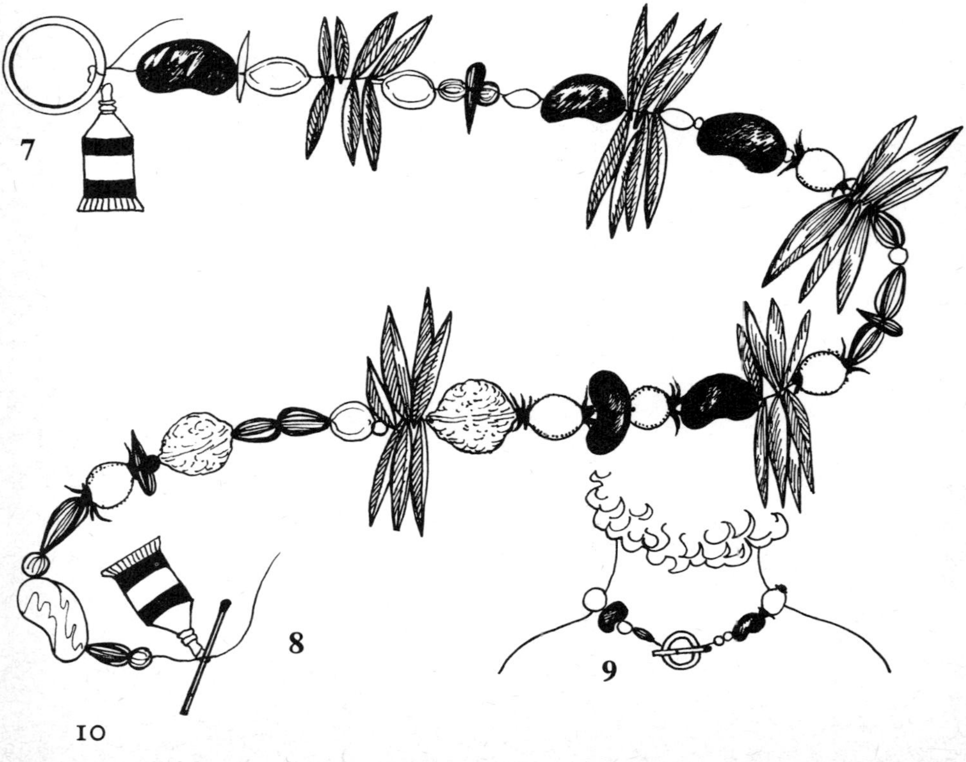

Your necklace may look different to those found in the jewelry shop, but it will be very similar to those beads worn by people in other parts of the world.

Tribal Jewelry

You need:
hollow bamboo or elder tree branches
hollow dried grasses
strong thread or fishing line
fine fuse wire
hammer and nail
assorted nuts (walnuts, brazils etc.)
chicken or fish bones
old teeth (if you can find them!)
small pieces of tree bark
old corks
feathers (long ones, found in the country
or taken from an old feather duster)
a small junior hacksaw

1 Saw the bamboo and elder into short lengths. You could sandpaper and varnish them if you like.

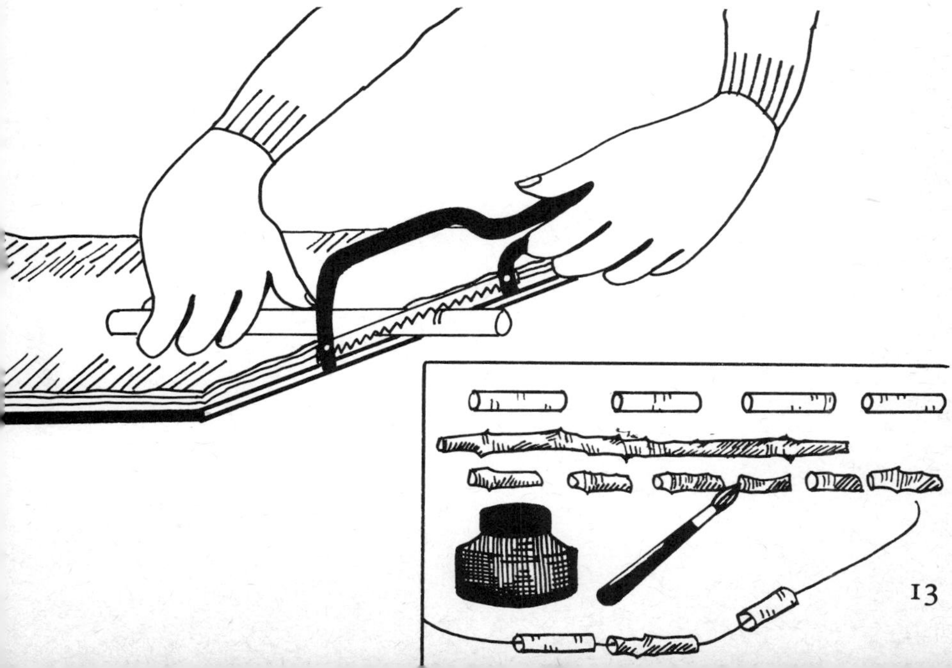

2 Wash the bones thoroughly and soak them overnight in bleach and water to make them whiter. Let them dry.

3 If you use nuts you will have to make a hole through them with a hand drill and vice, or you can use the special tool described in the seed pages and some plasticine.

4 Thread the items together in the order you choose, in the same way as for seeds and berries. Make a hole in the quill part of the feathers and the bones as you go along.

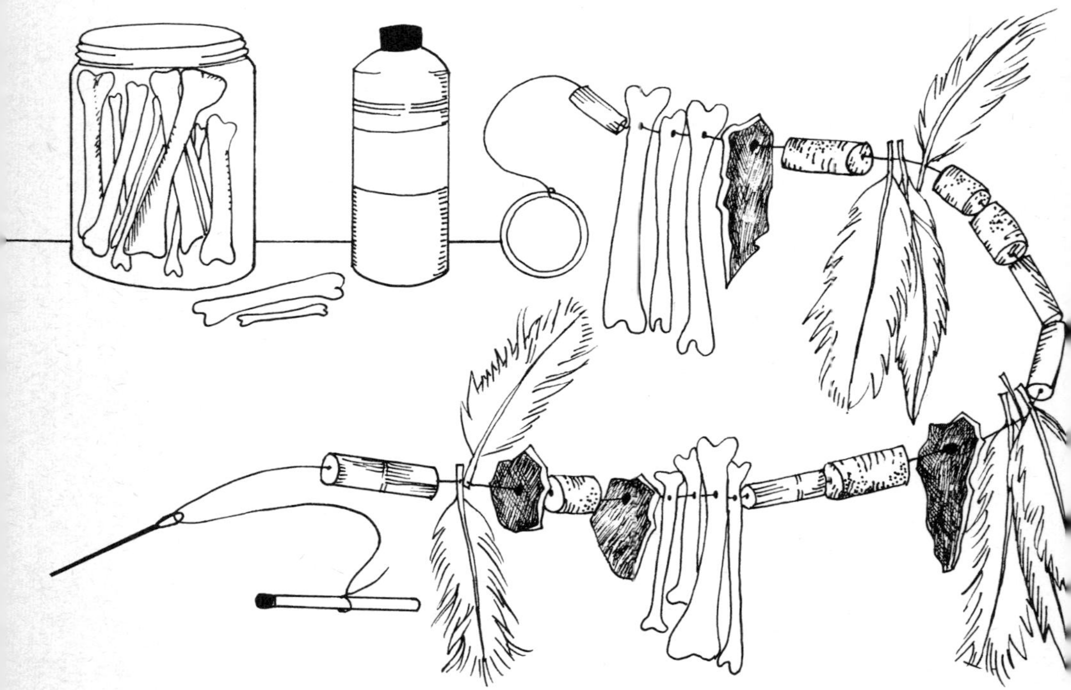

Add the finishing touch to your tribal jewelry by cutting a nose ring out of thin card.

1 Draw two small circles, one inside the other, and cut out the ring. Cut a slit through one side.

2 Bend the edges round to fit your nose. Curve them so that they fit comfortably.

Now you can be witch doctor, medicine man, or tribal chief just as you fancy. The bones, feathers, tree bark and so on that you are wearing often had a magic meaning besides, so you could try out a few voodoo spells.

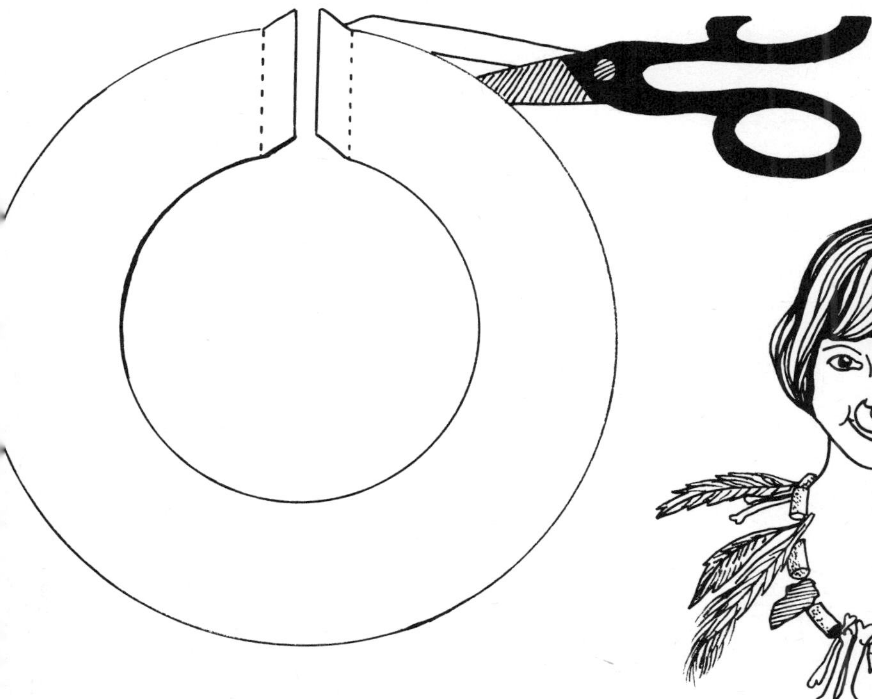

Pine cones and acorns

Look on the ground, as well as in the hedgerows and trees, to find just one small pine cone and a couple of acorns for some 'organic' jewelry.

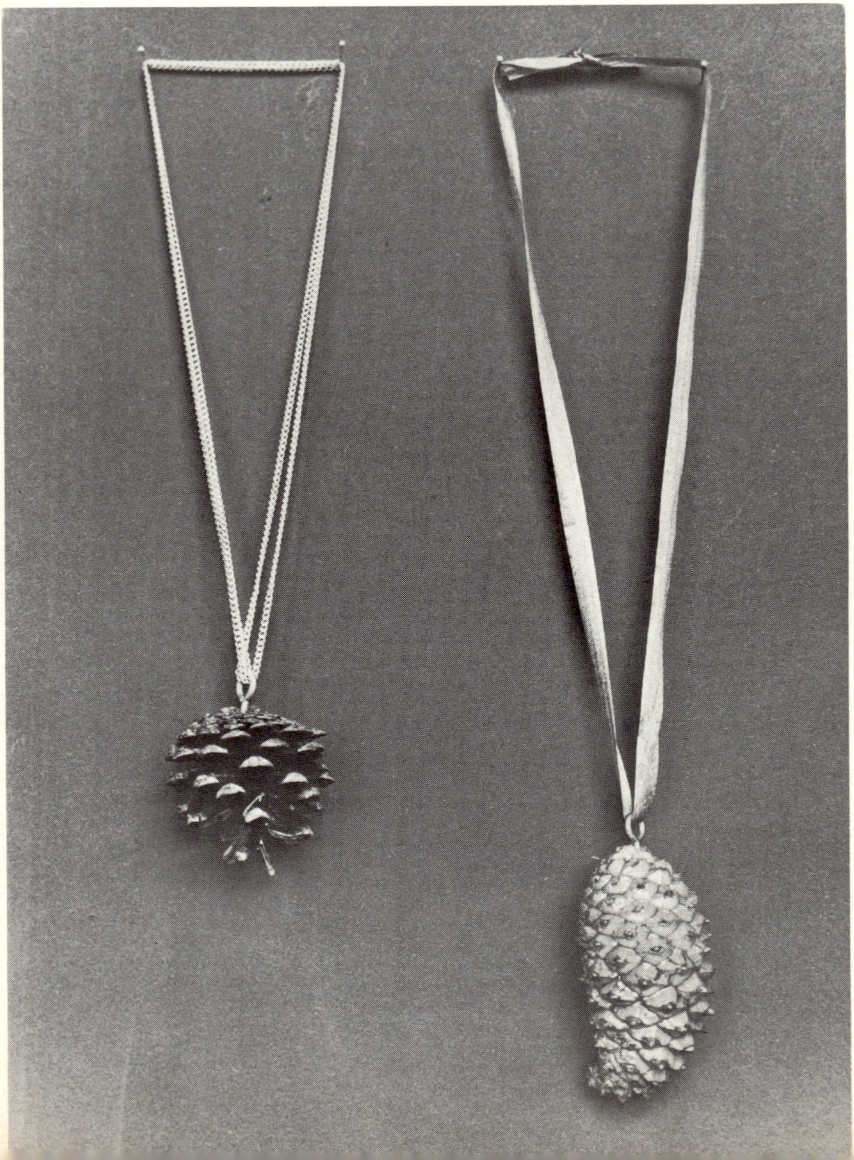

You also need:
varnish
a leather shoelace or thin chain
(like a plug chain)
a split curtain ring
an eyelet hook
2 screw earring fitments
tin foil, glue
fine fuse wire, pin or needle

1 Dry the pine cone and acorns in an airing cupboard and varnish them.

2 Screw the eyelet hook into the base of the cone.

3 Use an old leather shoelace or chain to hang it round your neck. If you use a chain, join the ends together with the split curtain ring.

Ask your mother if she has two old screw earrings she no longer wants. They do not have to be a pair, since all you will need to make the acorn earrings is the fitment part. Remove it carefully from the rest of the earring. Use pliers if it is difficult.

1 Cut two small circles out of tin foil and make a hole through the centres with a pin or needle.

2 Cut two short lengths of fuse wire. Crumple one end of each piece into a tiny ball and push the other end through the holes made in the tin foil circles.

3 Put some glue on top of the acorns and fold the tin foil circles over the ends to look like caps. The crumpled part of the wire should be on the inside.

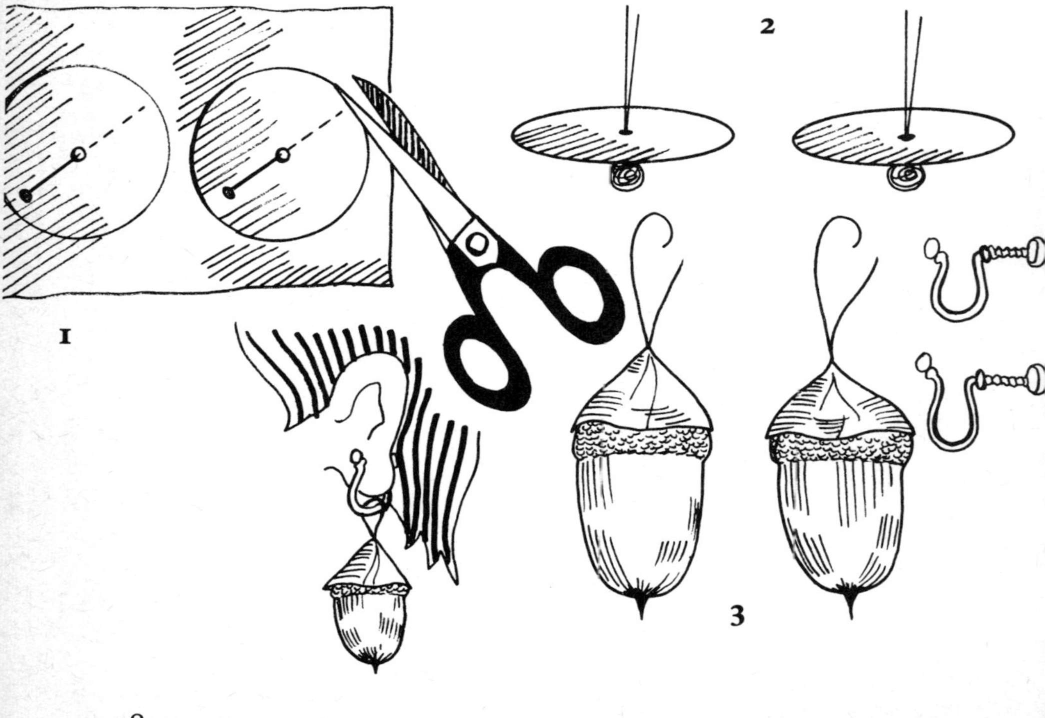

When the glue has set, pass the other ends of the wire round each of the earring fitments. Tie it on the wire and twist the ends together.

Hawaiian garland

Visitors to the tropical island of Hawaii are traditionally welcomed with a garland of flowers.

To make one of these colourful displays you need:
flowers (French marigolds, roses, daisies or any other firm headed flower).
grasses (pampas)
barley or oats
poppy seed heads
fishing line
green heavy paper
scissors
pencil
needle

1 Choose flowers that are in full colour and pick them on a dry day. Remove the leaves.

2 Tie the flowers in small bunches and hang them upside down in a dry and airy place – but not in direct sunlight. Leave them for a week, then off with their heads!

3 Fold the green paper in half. All along the fold draw the shapes of half a leaf (so that the fold is at the centre of the leaf) and cut them out.

4 Thread the fishing line through the centre of the flower heads and the leaves until you have enough for a large garland.

Next time your friends call round, give them a real Hawaiian welcome. You could perhaps wear a grass skirt too, made from coloured string, ribbons or raffia.

2

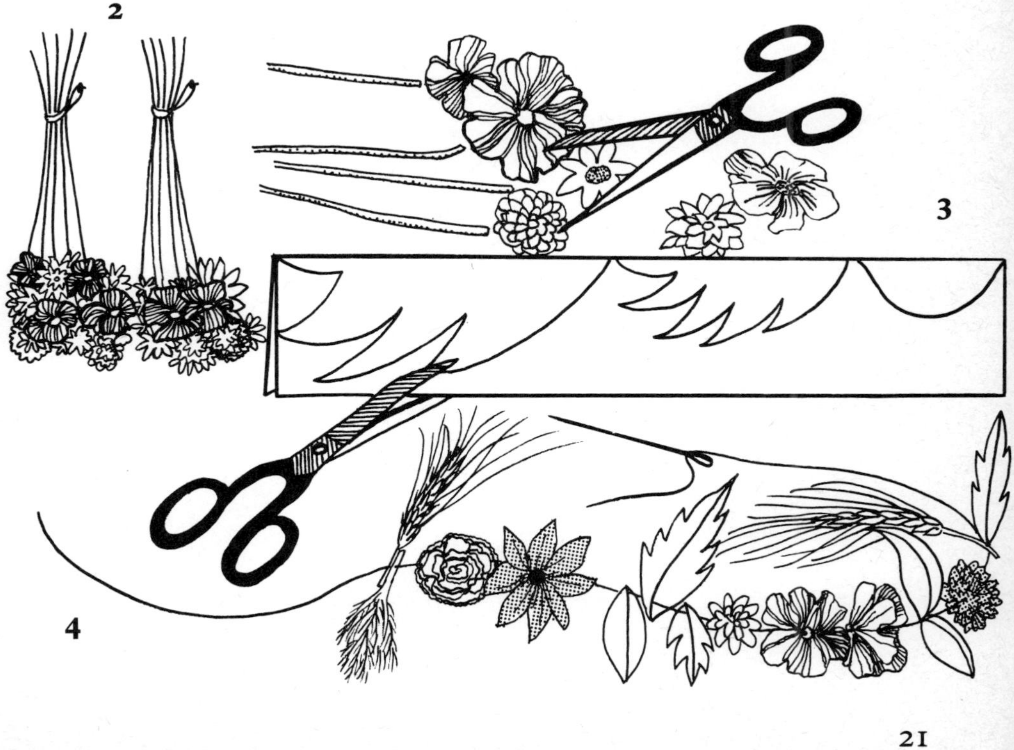

3

4

Grocery gems

A quick peek in some of the jars and packets in the kitchen cupboard can spark off many new ideas. Your next dinner might have a few less noodles or carrots in it, but your jewel box will certainly be fuller.

For a grocery necklace you can use some of these:
dried beans (black eyed, broad, coffee, red or butter beans)
dried peas (ordinary green or chick peas)
noodles; macaroni; raisins etc.
coloured plastic drinking straws

1 Some of the dried beans may need soaking overnight. Test them with a needle first to see if you can pierce them.

2 Cut the drinking straws into short lengths.

3 Tie and glue a curtain ring to the end of some thread in the same way as before (page 10).

4 Thread up your necklace. Some of the straws can hang down if you push the needle through the end instead of passing it down the middle.

5 When it is long enough to hang well round your neck, cut the thread and tie a matchstick at the end. Secure it with a blob of glue in the same way as the ring.

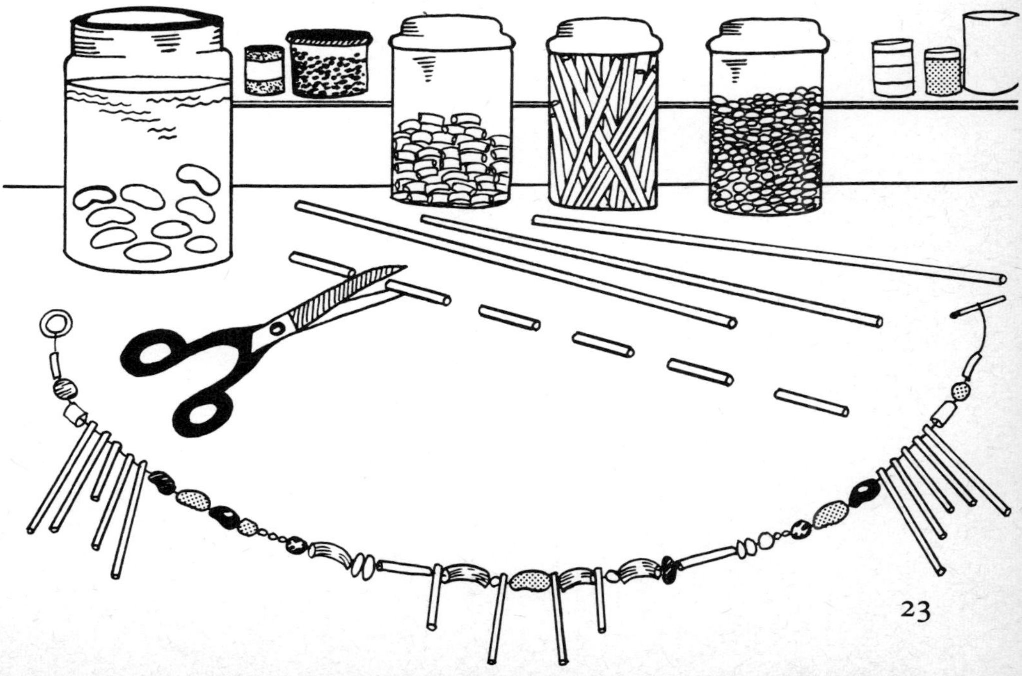

The vegetable rack and sweet tin can also be raided for a whole set of 'tasty' jewels for a little brother or sister.

You need:
a length of shirring elastic
a large needle
kitchen knife
a selection of sweets (liquorice allsorts, fruit gums, dolly mixtures, Polos, jelly babies etc.)
scissors
2 large carrots
some radishes
4 hard cherries (in pairs)
puffed wheat
vegetable dye

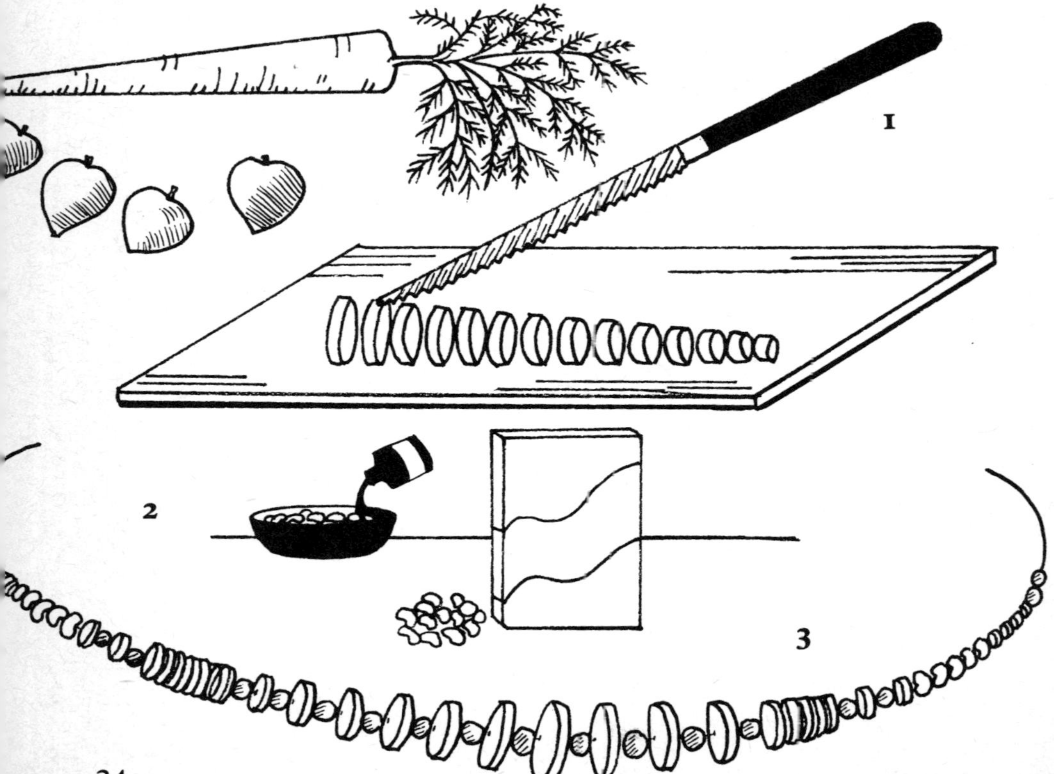

1 For the first course, peel, wash and dry the carrots and cut them into slices on a kitchen cutting board. Start at the bigger end and make the slices thinner as you go along. Wash and dry the radishes.

2 Colour some puffed wheat with vegetable dye and let it dry.

3 Thread the elastic through the needle and pierce the vegetables and wheat, plus a few raisins perhaps. Arrange the carrots in order of size.

4 For the second course, thread the elastic and start joining all the sweets together in a bracelet. When it is big enough – remember that the elastic will stretch over the child's hand – cut it and tie knots at both ends. Tie the ends together and slip it on.

5 For the perfect dessert make a pair of real cherry earrings. All you do is pop them over your sister's ears. Remind her to save the stones for you, though!

4

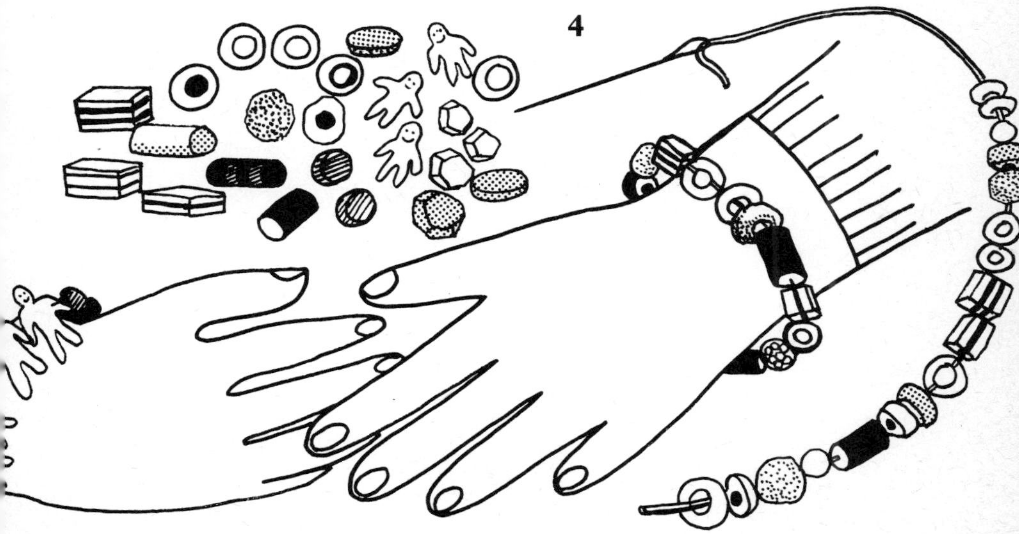

Pebbles

Collecting can be half the fun of making jewelry from pebbles and sea shells. Believe it or not, you can still find semi-precious stones like amethysts and cornelians on the beaches, but they take a lot of searching for.

You will easily discover lots of other colourful pebbles, though. Take those whose shape and colour appeal to you and wash and scrub them when you get home. Varnish them when they are dry.

To make a pebble neck band you need:
2 leather shoelaces (or leather thongs)
strong glue
some small pebbles (about the same size as each other)
fuse wire

1 Spread some newspaper on the table.

2 Place the two leather shoelaces beside each other on the table. Arrange the stones in between them in the order you want (see page 28). Leave space at each end.

3 Glue along the side of one shoelace. Stick it to each of the stones in turn so that they all lie next to each other (see page 28) but without touching.

4 When the glue has set, do the same thing on the other side. Glue the two shoelaces together where they meet between the pebbles and at the ends. Leave it to dry.

5 Tie and bind fine fuse wire round the leather between the pebbles. This will make the neck band stronger.

6 Tie the band together round your neck.

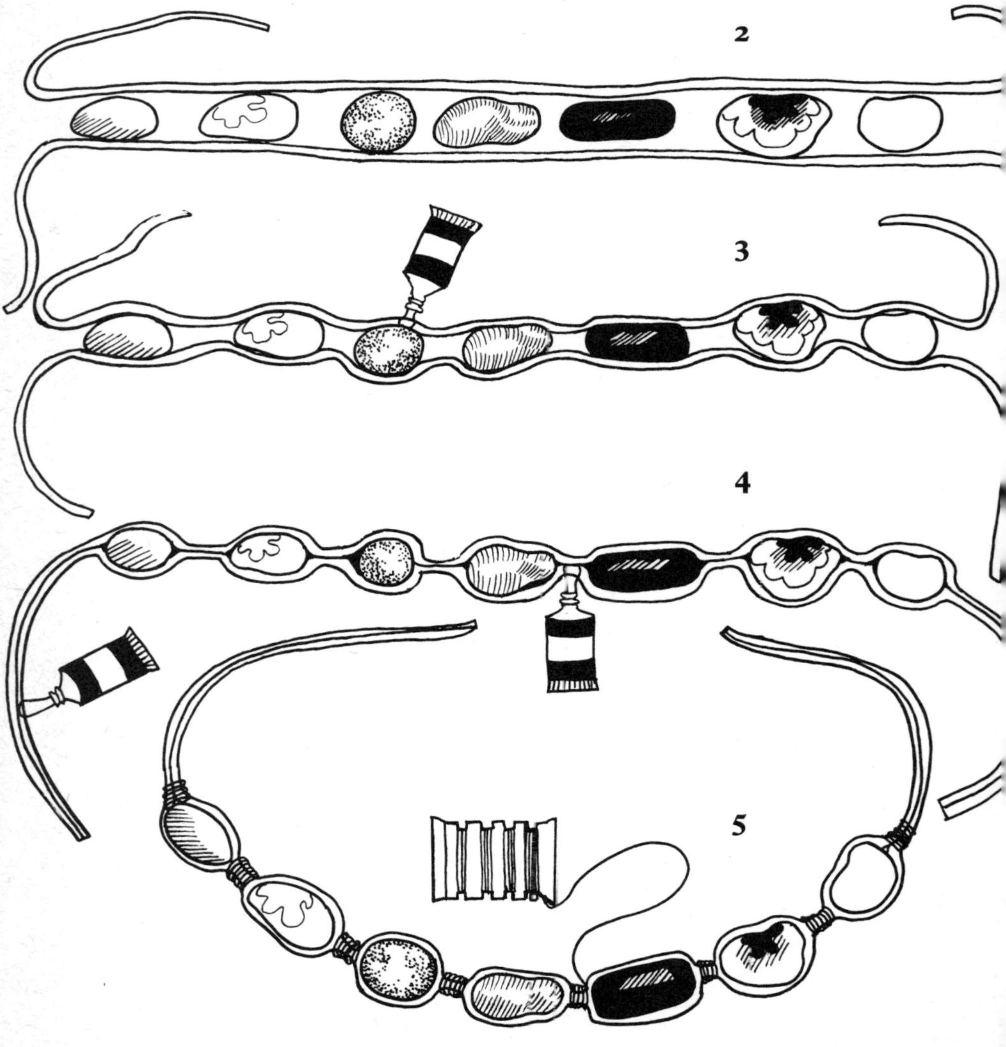

Pebbles can also be set in a ring or hung as pendants using thicker (30 amp) fuse wire (or ordinary wire without the plastic insulation).

To make a cradle for the pebble:
1 Cut two pieces of wire about three times longer than the pebble. Twist them together in a cross on the table and add a dab of glue where they meet.

2 When the glue has set, place the pebble end up at the centre of the cross and carefully lift up the four ends. Twist them round and round and into a loop.

3 Cut another bit of wire and make a sort of belt round the middle by twisting it round each of the other wires in turn.

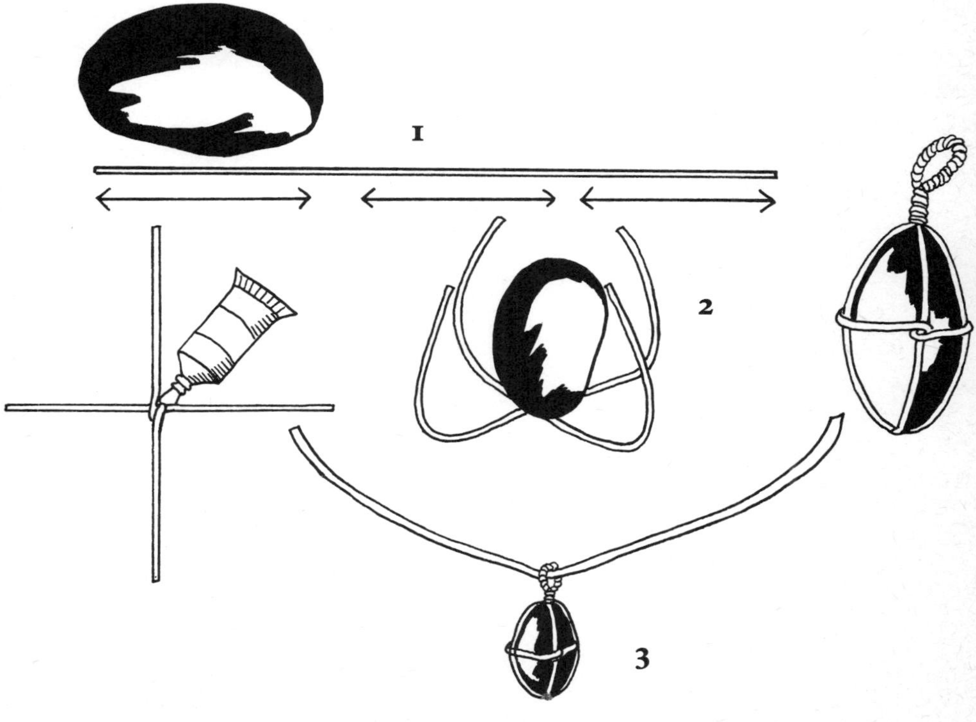

The pebble is now ready for hanging. If you find pebbles with holes already in them you can of course just thread them straight round your neck. And these types of stones are said to be especially lucky.

To make a claw ring:
1 Twist two short lengths of wire into one. Leave the ends open. Fold the wire round so that the loose ends meet.

2 Shape the wire into a ring to fit your finger by twisting it round and round with some pliers to make the hole smaller.

3 Put some glue on the end of the stone and place it in between the four wires. Fold them over so that they grip the ring like a claw.

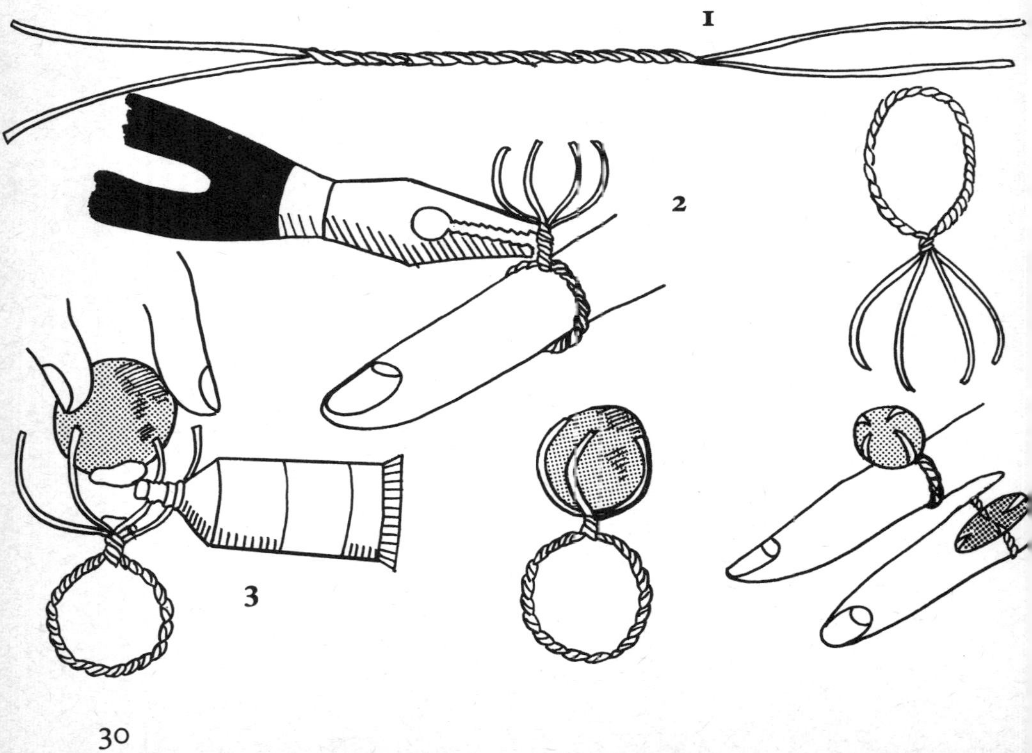

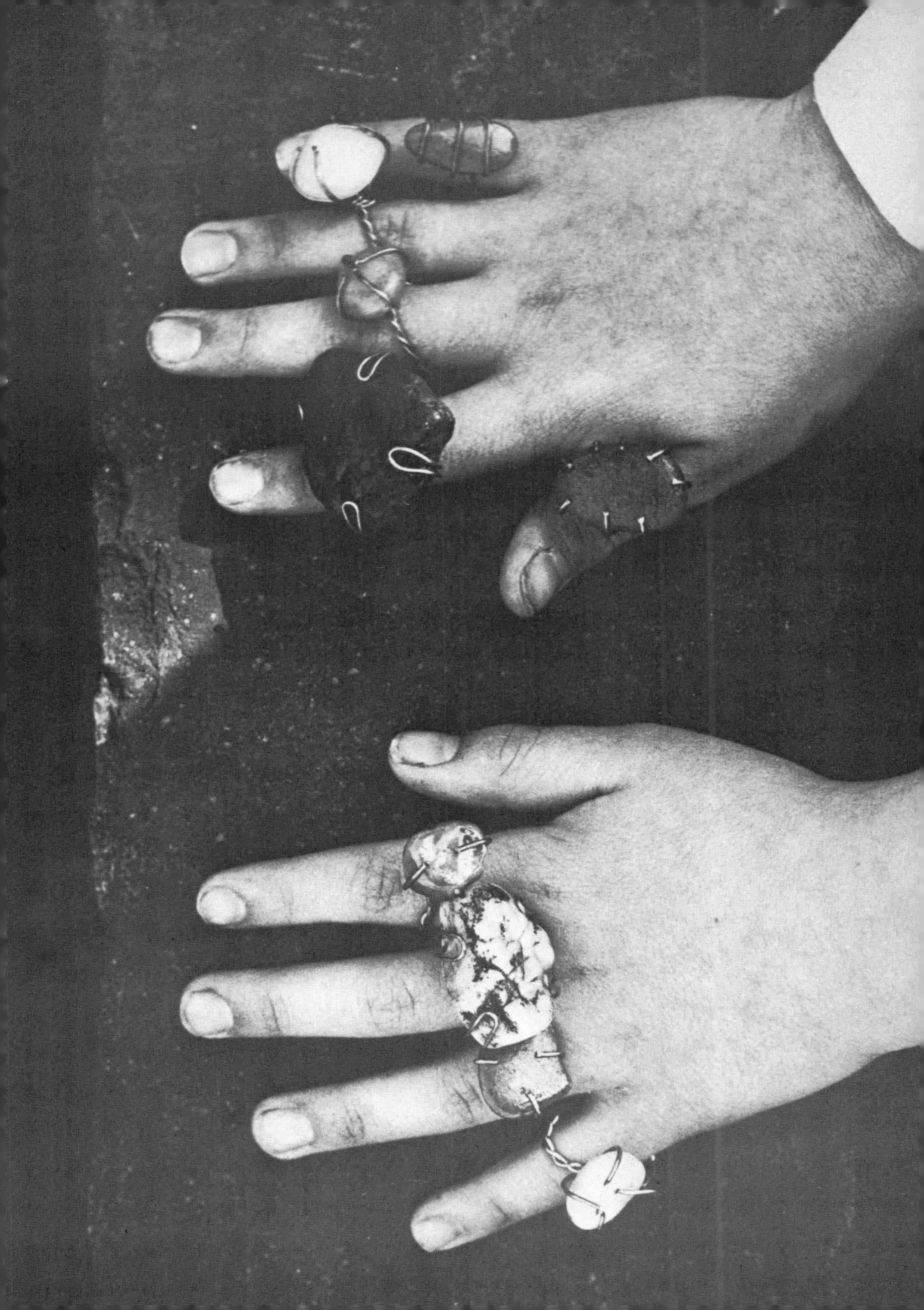

Shell jewel box

Shells were once used as money in Polynesia and parts of North America. But you do not have to look that far away; many kinds of shells can be found on your nearest beach if you look carefully. Collect a variety – cockles, mussels, winkles, and so on – and ask if anyone has an old cigar box to spare.

Opposite A variety of necklaces made from berries, seeds, pips and stones (see page 7), all very colourful and simple to make

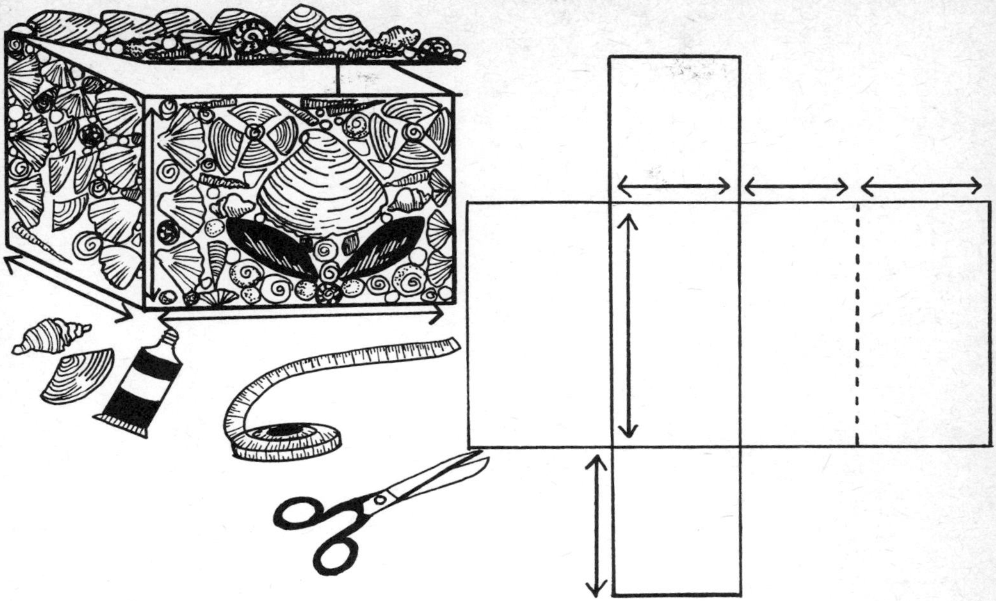

1 Wash and dry the shells. Sort them out and arrange them as you want them to appear on the box. If you find some sea glass, this would look nice too.

2 Glue the shells to the sides and top of the cigar box.

3 Line the box with some felt, velvet or satin to give the box a look of luxury. Measure the length, width and depth of the box and cut out a pattern like the one shown in the diagram. Cut the fabric to the pattern and glue it to the inside of the box.

Shells can be made into other types of jewelry. If you have any left over after making your jewel box, use them in necklaces, bracelets, brooches and even in rings.

Opposite Some 'tasty' jewels (see page 24) of fruit, sweets and vegetables

Macramé belt

Sailors and fishermen have passed on their knotting skills over the years. Other people have turned their knowledge into something decorative as well as useful. Twine, cord and most of the kinds of string you find lying around the house can be used in macramé, the art of knotting.

You also need:
a rectangular piece of hardboard or thick card (about one meter long)
tacks
hammer
scissors
beads, buttons, nuts and washers

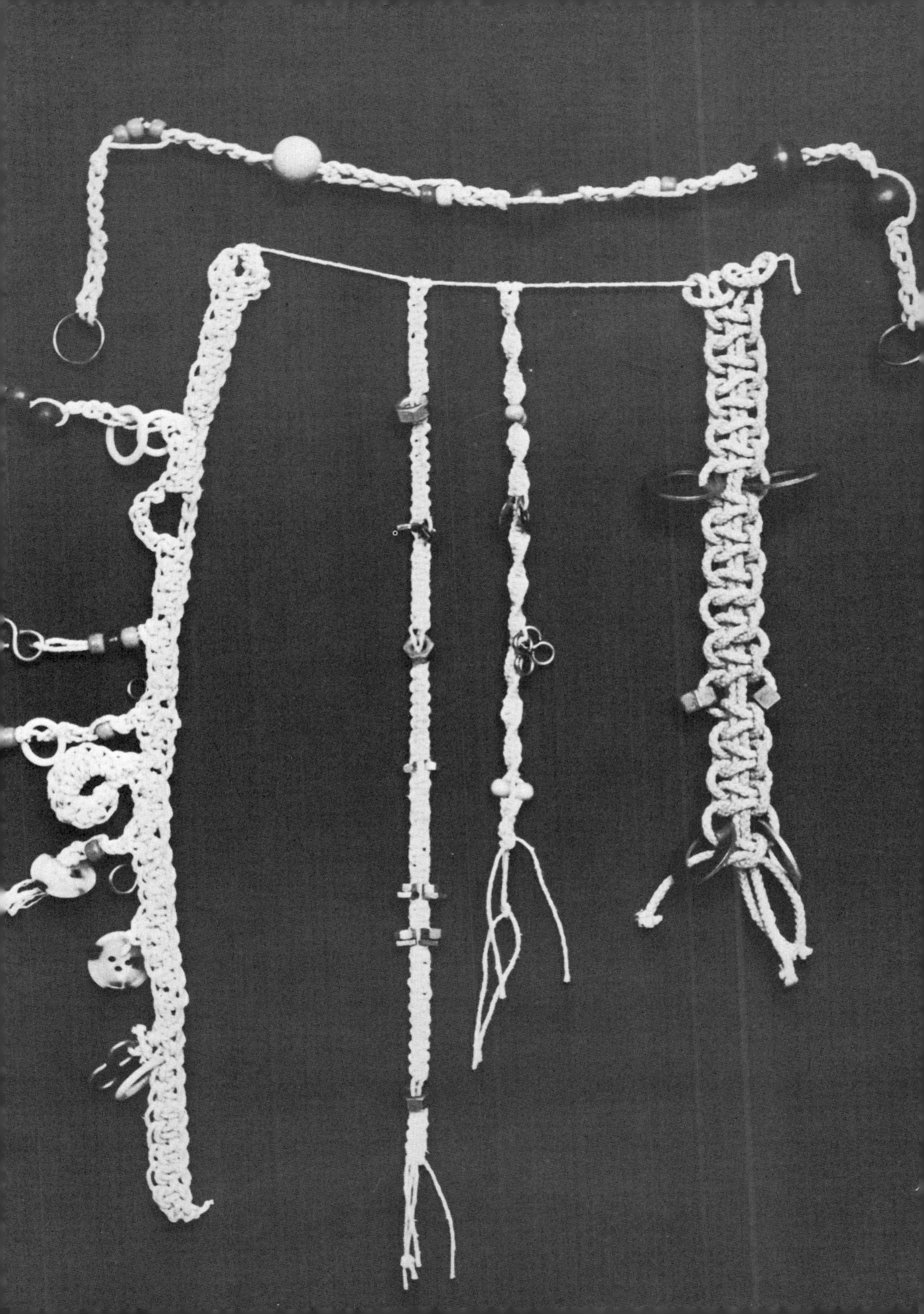

1 Cut a short piece of cord and tie two small loops at each end. Fix it across the top of the board with two tacks. This is called the holding cord. Hammer another tack into the bottom of the board.

2 Cut two pieces of cord four metres long. Fold each length round the holding cord and tie a 'lark's head' knot in the way shown in the diagram. It is important that the two outside lengths of cord (black and white in the diagram) are much longer than those on the inside (shaded in the diagram) when they hang from the holding cord. Make the outside cords three metres long and those on the inside one metre.

3 Pass the two inside lengths round the tack at the bottom of the board and tie them together.

4 The two outside lengths are known as your working cords. To make a macramé belt you must knot these round the two centre cords. Follow the diagrams **a**, **b** and **c** closely to see how the knots are made. Keep repeating the knot.

5 As the belt grows it will spiral round. You can add beads and washers to the outer cords as you go along. When the cord has been used up, tie the lower four ends to four beads to stop fraying. Remove the holding cord from the board, add a few beads, and tie the ends together. This is called the half-knot method.

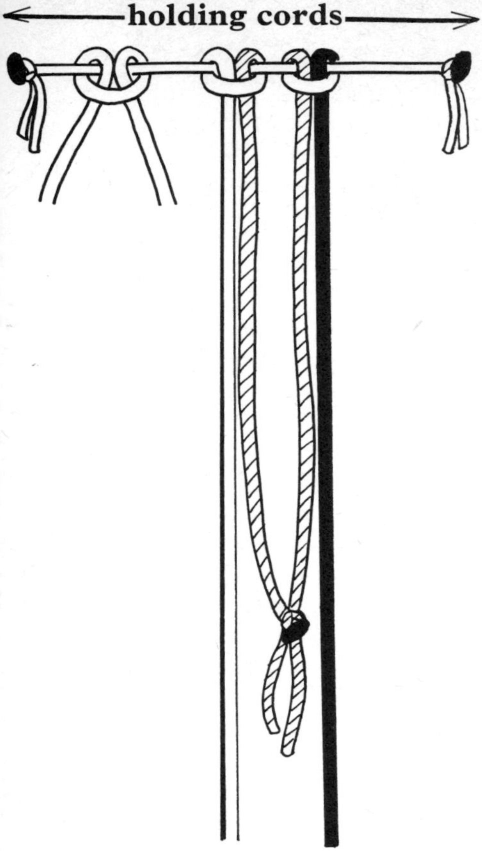

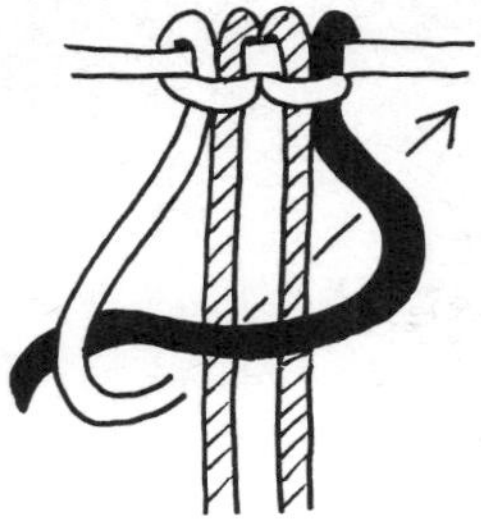

a

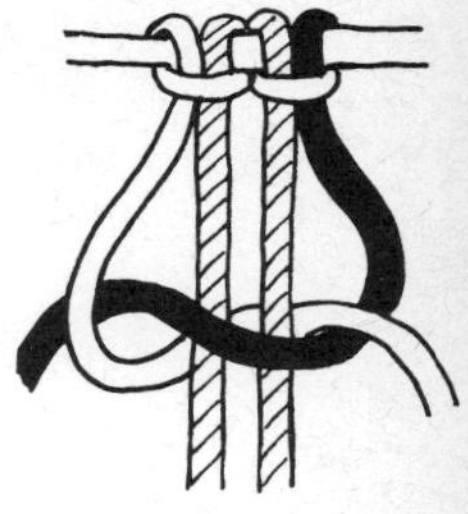

b

c

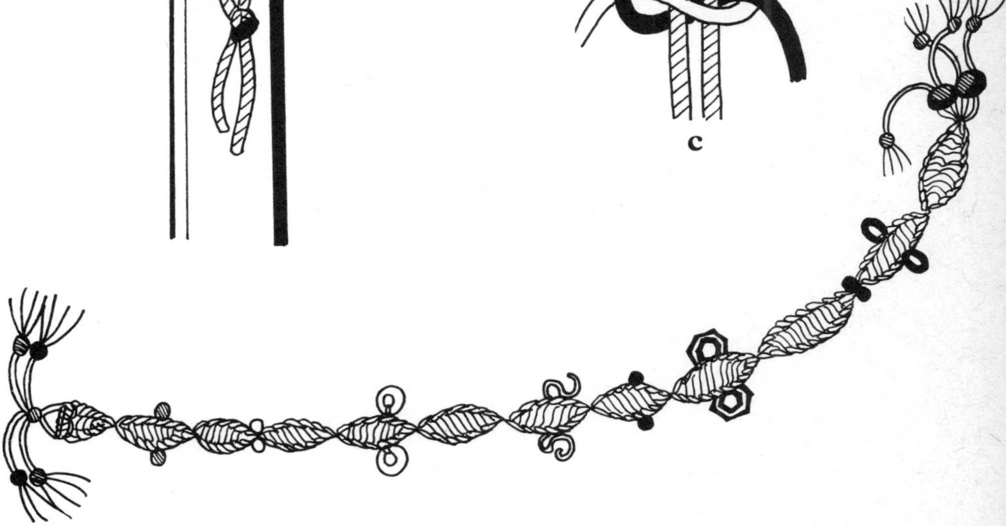

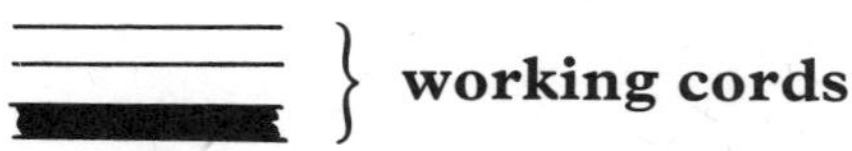

To make a flat, rather than a spiral, belt you will have to use a square knot, but it is very similar.

1 Start in the same way as before by fixing a holding cord onto the board and attaching the longer cords by a lark's head knot. The lengths used are exactly the same as before and the two centre pieces are also tied round the tack at the bottom of the board.

2 Make one half knot **a**. Then follow the diagrams **b c d** to see exactly how the square knot is made. Add beads and other ornaments as you go, **e**. Finish off as before.

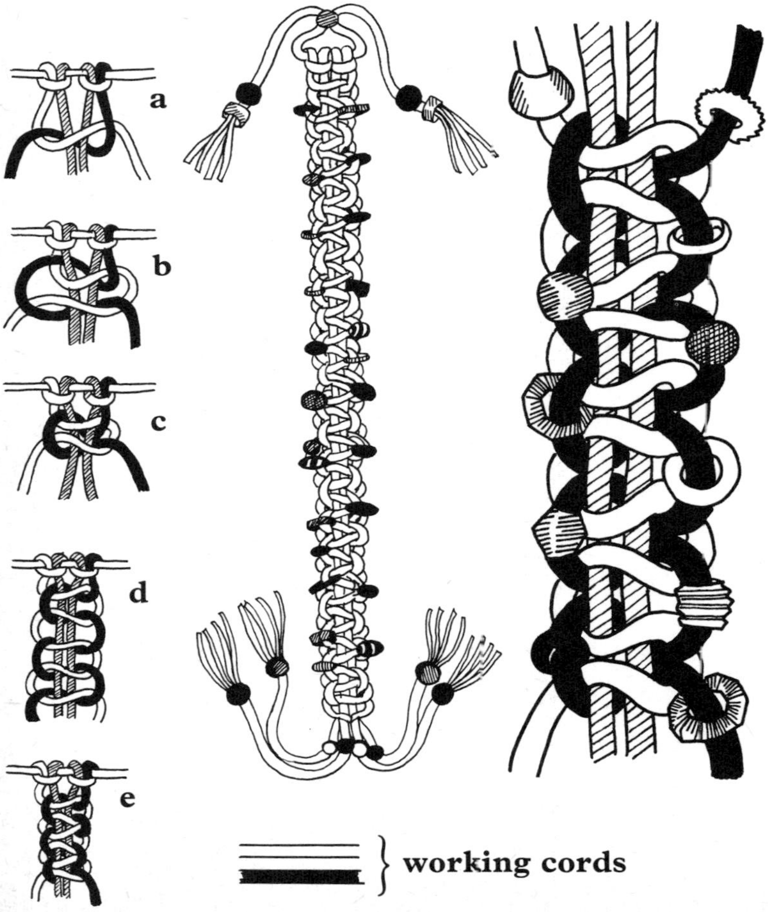

Try using much thicker cord to make more chunky types of belt. Although you macramé them in the same way they will look very different, especially if you add large nuts, beads and washers.

You may also like to try crocheting a belt (or a neckband) with wool, or plaiting one from ribbons or embroidery cotton. Include some sequins, real or home made, for a really glamorous effect.

There is a colour photograph of both a crocheted and a plaited belt on page 52.

Junk pendants

A very strange looking pendant can be made from a small alarm clock – a broken one, that is.

You need:
an old alarm clock, a small screwdriver, fuse wire, Araldite glue, a leather shoelace, pliers, the glass clock face or a jam jar lid

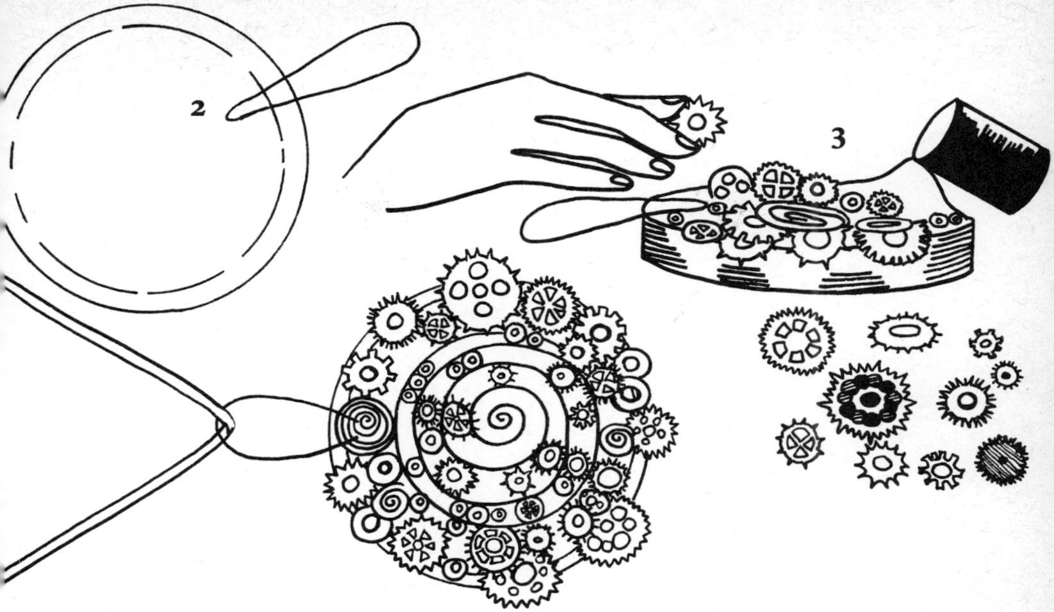

1 Carefully take the alarm clock to bits with a small screwdriver and pliers.

2 Make a small loop out of fuse wire and lay it on the inside of the glass face or jam jar lid so that the loop itself sticks out over the edge.

3 Holding the loop in place, fill up the inside of the glass with Araldite (following the instructions on the packet). Arrange the small pieces from the clock – the tiny springs, cogs and so on – in the Araldite. Leave everything to set.

After a couple of days, when the Araldite has hardened, thread an old leather shoelace through the loop and hang the pendant round your neck. You now have a perfect jewel for the Age of Technology.

If you do not happen to have an old clock lying around, the pieces taken from a thrown away transistor radio can look just as interesting.

You need:
a jam jar lid, hammer and nail, a leather shoelace, Polyfilla, and lots of transistor pieces

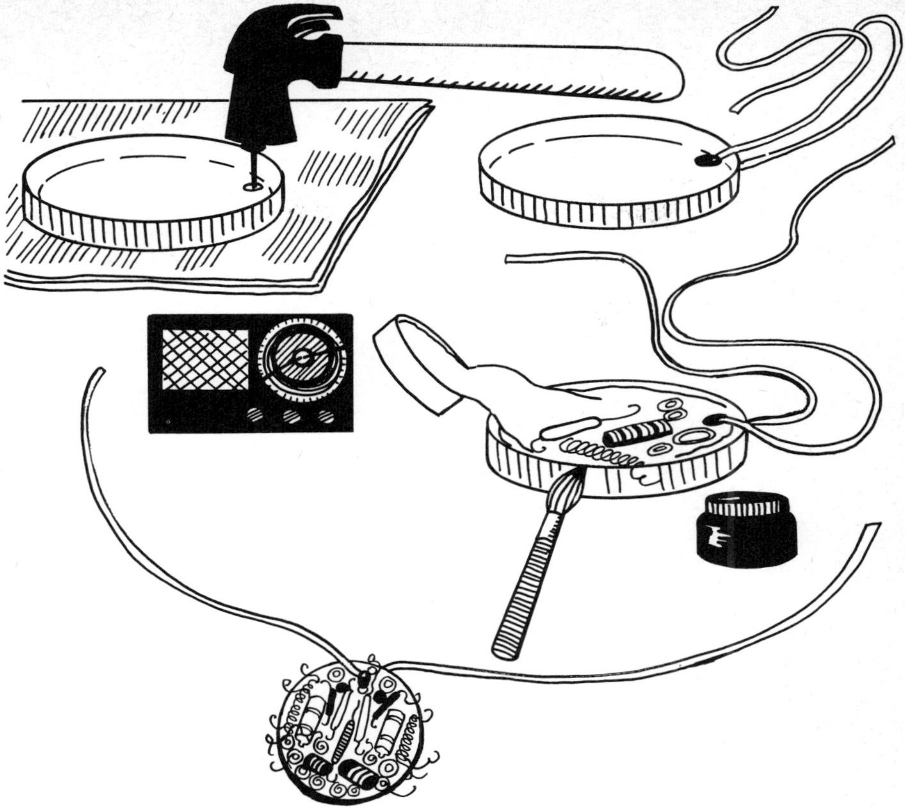

1 Use the hammer and nail to make a hole in the jam jar lid, near the edge. Do this on a workbench, or put several layers of newspaper down to avoid damaging the kitchen table.

2 Thread the shoelace through the hole.

3 Mix up just enough Polyfilla to fill up the lid, and pour it in. Just before the Polyfilla begins to set hard, arrange and fit in the radio parts. When it is hard, paint the Polyfilla and then hang the pendant round your neck.

Op art earrings

Ears must not be forgotten in your jewelry making. For big 'Op art' earrings you need just two jam jar lids, some black and white paint, fine fuse wire and a hammer and nail.

1 Make a hole in each lid, near the edge, with the hammer and nail.

2 Paint the lids with black and white 'optical' patterns, such as a bull's eye, a spiral, or a wheel. Leave them to dry.

3 Twist loops of fuse wire through the holes and hang them over your ears.

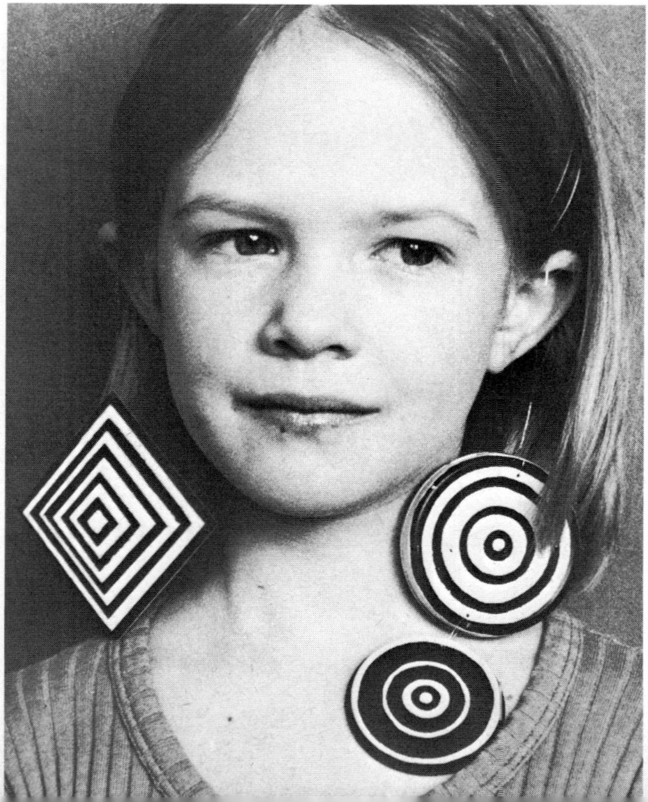

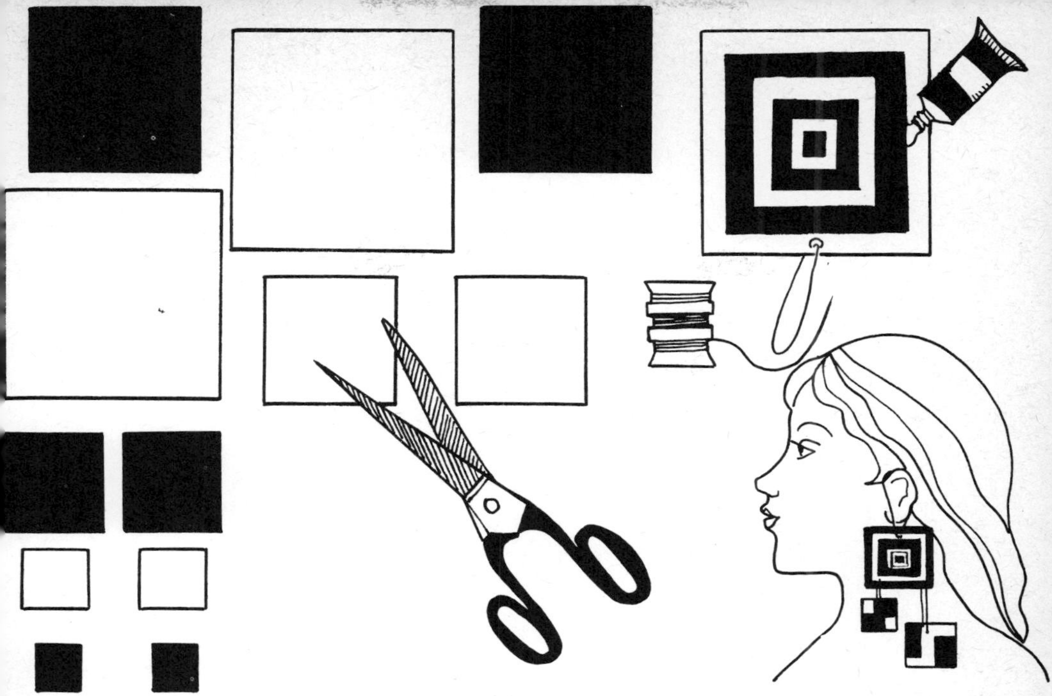

You could make other Op art earrings using nuts, bolts and washers, or even simple black and white card.

1 Cut the card into a number of different sized squares.

2 Glue the squares together, one on top of the other, in two piles. Put the largest ones at the bottom of the pile and the smallest on top. Change the colour at each step.

3 Make a hole with a needle on the edge of the two bottom squares (the biggest) and thread some fuse wire through.

Before wearing them you might like to add on another stage with more fuse wire so that they really dangle. These sorts of shapes and patterns are guaranteed to dazzle the eyes.

Hands and feet jewelry

Have you ever seen a belly dancer swaying to the music, her hands and feet tinkling with the jewelry she wore? You can make some musical jewelry from old plug, padlock or dog chains, some curtain rings, and bells. You will also need pliers, leather shoe-laces, and small safety pins.

1 Make four chain bands; two for your wrists and two for your ankles. Open the chain links with the pliers and use small safety pins to join the bands together.

2 Divide the rest of the chain into sixteen lengths. Eight of them should be long enough to reach from your wrist to the middle of your fingers, **a**, and the other eight from your ankle to your toes **b**.

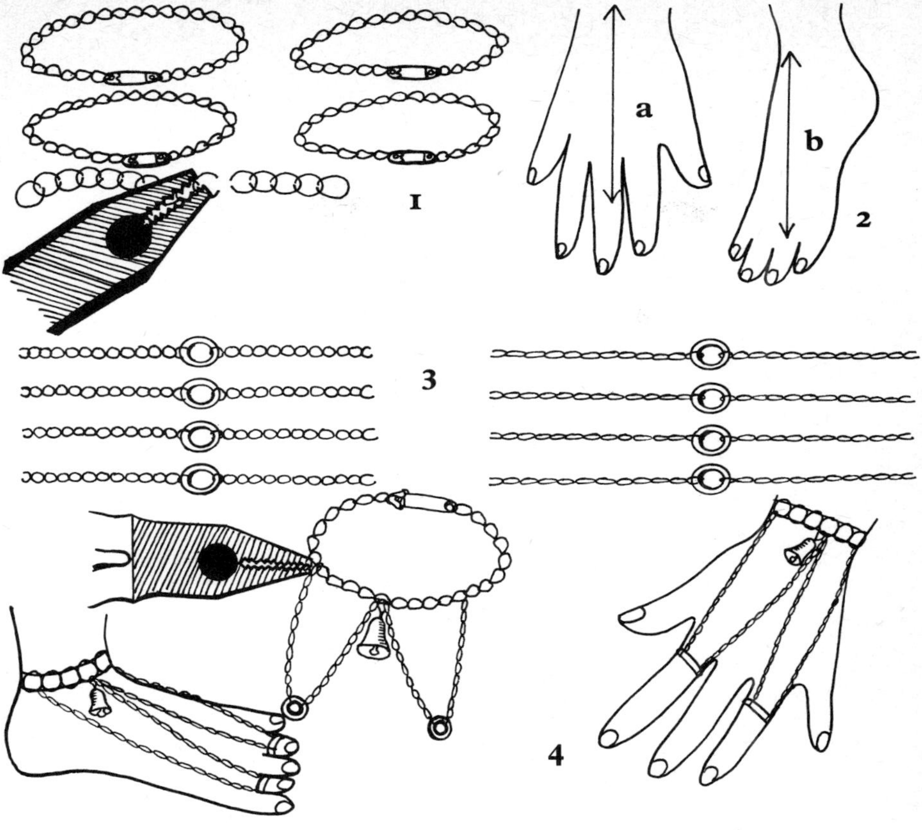

3 Join the chains in pairs with eight curtain rings.

4 Now attach the other ends to each of the wrist and ankle bands, so that each one has two loops.

5 Add the bells to the links. Thread the shoelaces in and out of the links of the wrist and ankle bands.

Dress up in the musical jewelry by putting on the bands and pushing your fingers and toes through the curtain rings. Now switch on some exotic music and dance away.

Copper wire jewelry

Look for your next source of ideas in your tool box and the local hardware store.

You need these tools:
file
snub nose and cutting pliers (tin snips if possible)
emery paper

You also need:
steel wool
pencil
a large washer with a small hole in the middle
a nail
lots of copper wire (or electric cable with the insulating plastic scraped off with pliers)

On the facing page are just a few of the different necklaces and bracelets you could make with copper wire.

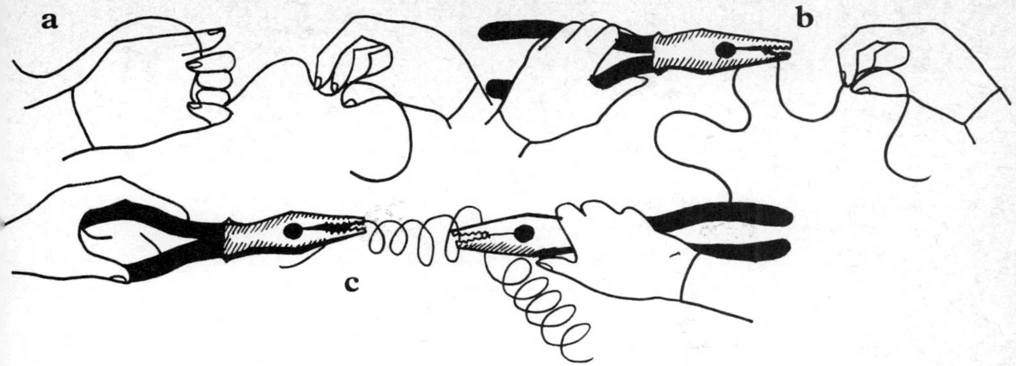

The main ways of bending and shaping wire are:

a using your fingers to make large soft bends
b using pliers and fingers
c using two pairs of pliers – one pair to hold the wire and the other to twist it with

More complicated shapes are not too difficult to make once you know a few tricks of the trade.

To make a **switchback** design flatten some heavier gauge wire with a hammer before bending it into shape. Thread beads or seeds onto it for a necklace.

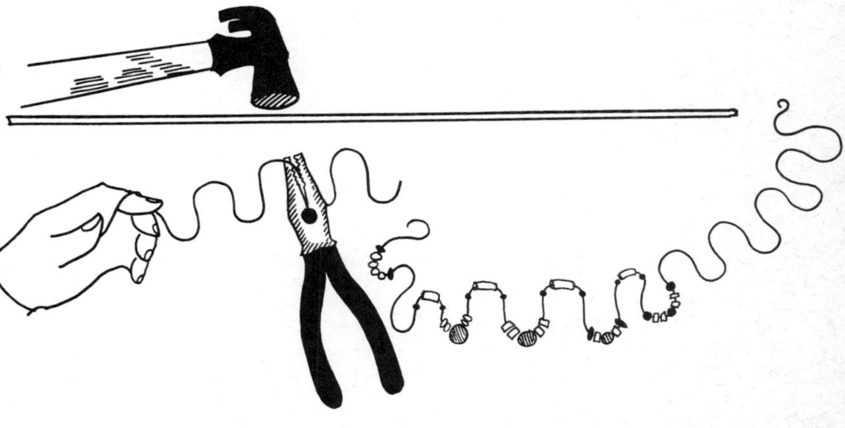

Opposite Use your own ideas for a crocheted or plaited belt or try your hand at simple macramé (see page 36)

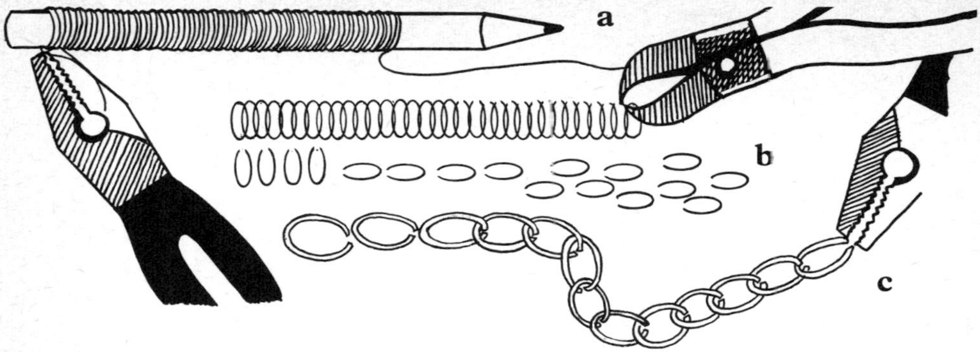

Jump rings are decorative and can be used as links. Bend the wire round a pencil, **a** (use pliers to make it tight). Pull the pencil out and cut along one side with tin snips, **b**. The rings can be linked by gently closing them round each other with pliers, **c**. You can then complete the circle when you have enough for a bracelet or necklace.

Make rings round different sized objects – a knitting needle, the handle of a wooden kitchen spoon, a candle, and so on – to make your jewelry more interesting. Store each size in its own special matchbox.

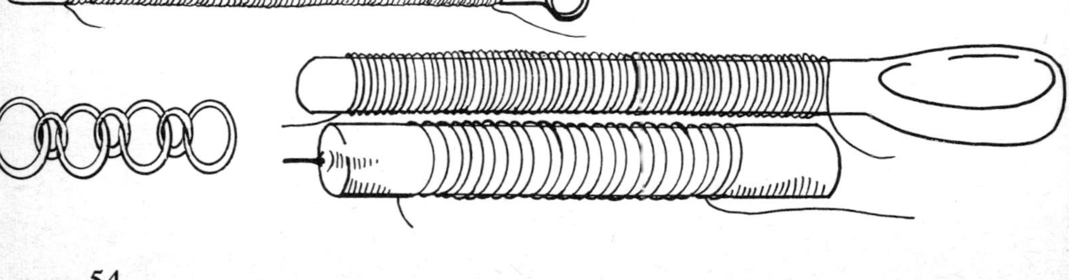

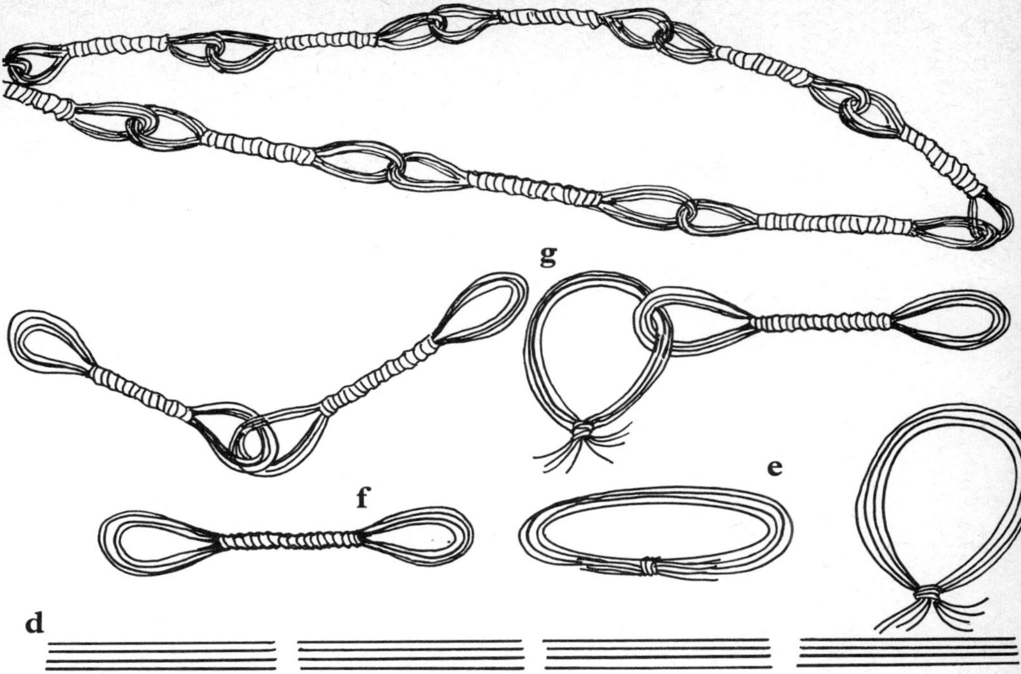

Twisted wire loops make an attractive necklace. If you have some very fine copper wire, cut it up into equal lengths and divide them into groups of four or five strands each, **d**.

Make one of the groups into a ring by twisting the ends together, **e**.

Squeeze the ring into a long shape and twist it so that there is a loop at each end, **f**.

Now thread the next group of wires through one of the loops and do the same as before, **g**.

Continue joining all the groups in this way until you have a chain long enough for a necklace. Join up the ends and put it over your head.

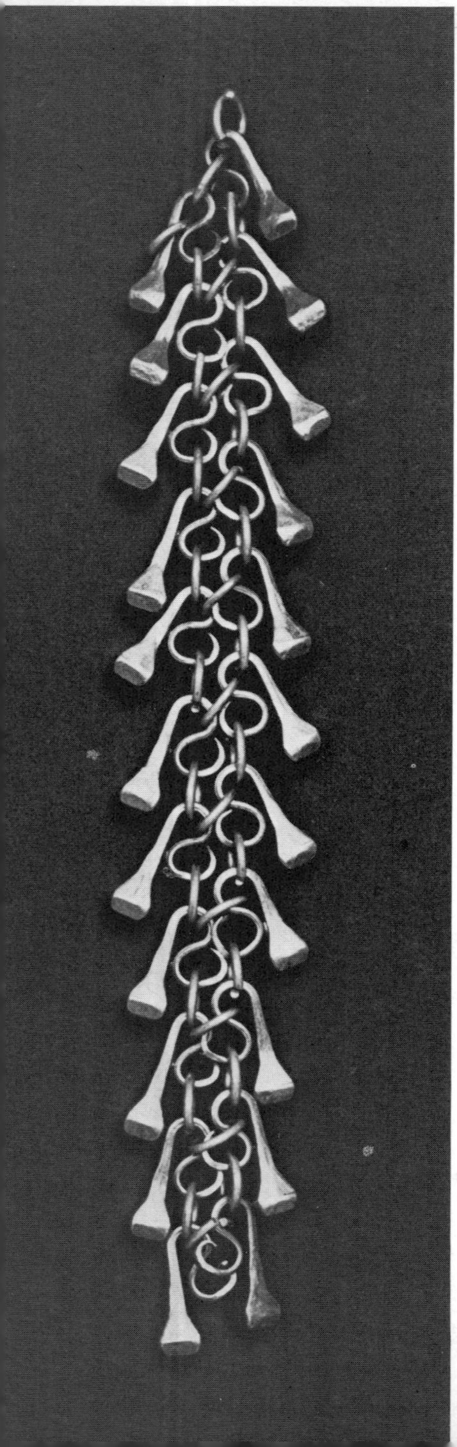

Now try out some of your own ideas for 'tool box' jewelry.

You could bend some nails into 'snake' patterns and join them together with wire links. In order to bend a nail into a snake you will have to bend it with pliers round a fat nail or bolt. Bend one half of the snake at a time.

Or you could join washers and nuts together with wire to make an unusual pendant.

File off any sharp points or edges of the wire or nails and smooth them with emery paper. Use steel wool to shine the jewelry. You could perhaps add some beads to your designs to make them look more professional.

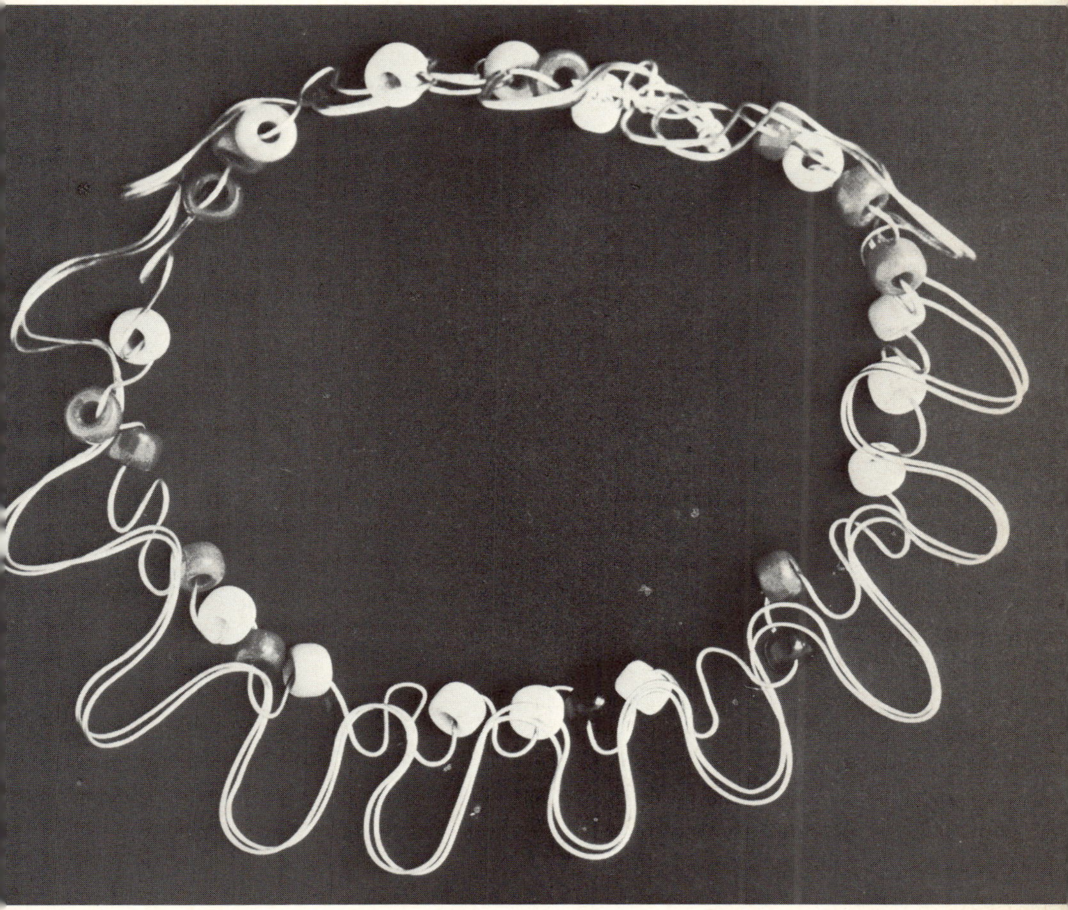

Initial brooch

You need:
thick card, pencil, Sellotape, safety pin, scissors, glitter, glue, tiddlywinks, old beads and buttons

1 Draw and cut your initial out of the card. Make it big and fat so that everyone can see it.

2 Attach a safety pin to one side of the card with Sellotape. Make sure that the pin part is free to move.

3 On the other side of the card glue the whole surface and then stick on the glitter, tiddlywinks, beads and buttons in whatever pattern you like. Leave it to dry and then pin it on your sweater. Let everyone try to guess your name.

There are a lot of other brooch ideas. You may like to make a fish or star shape, for instance. You could also attach an old hair slide to the back, instead of the safety pin.

Beads from paper

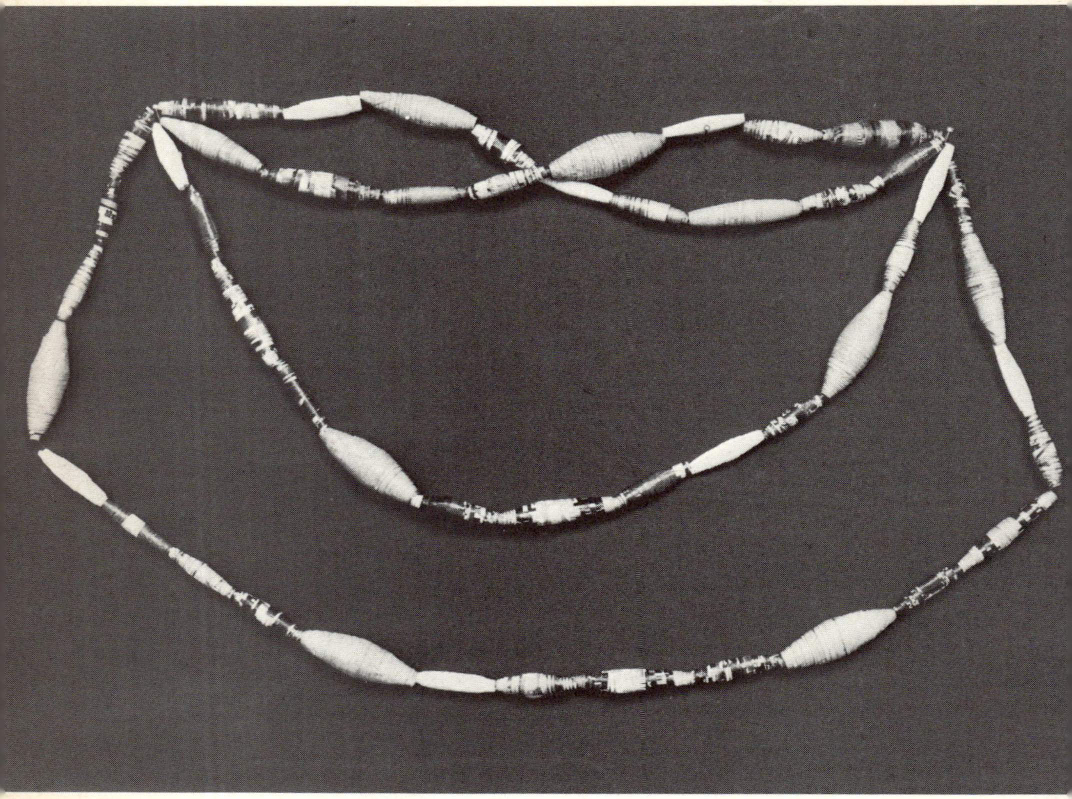

Odd scraps of paper found in the waste paper basket can be fashioned into attractive beads.

1 Mix up some cold water paste (or make it from equal amounts of laundry starch and water).

2 Cut the paper into long, triangular strips, paste them and wrap them round a knitting needle. When they have dried, remove the needle to leave the hole.

3 Paint the beads in bright colours and varnish them.

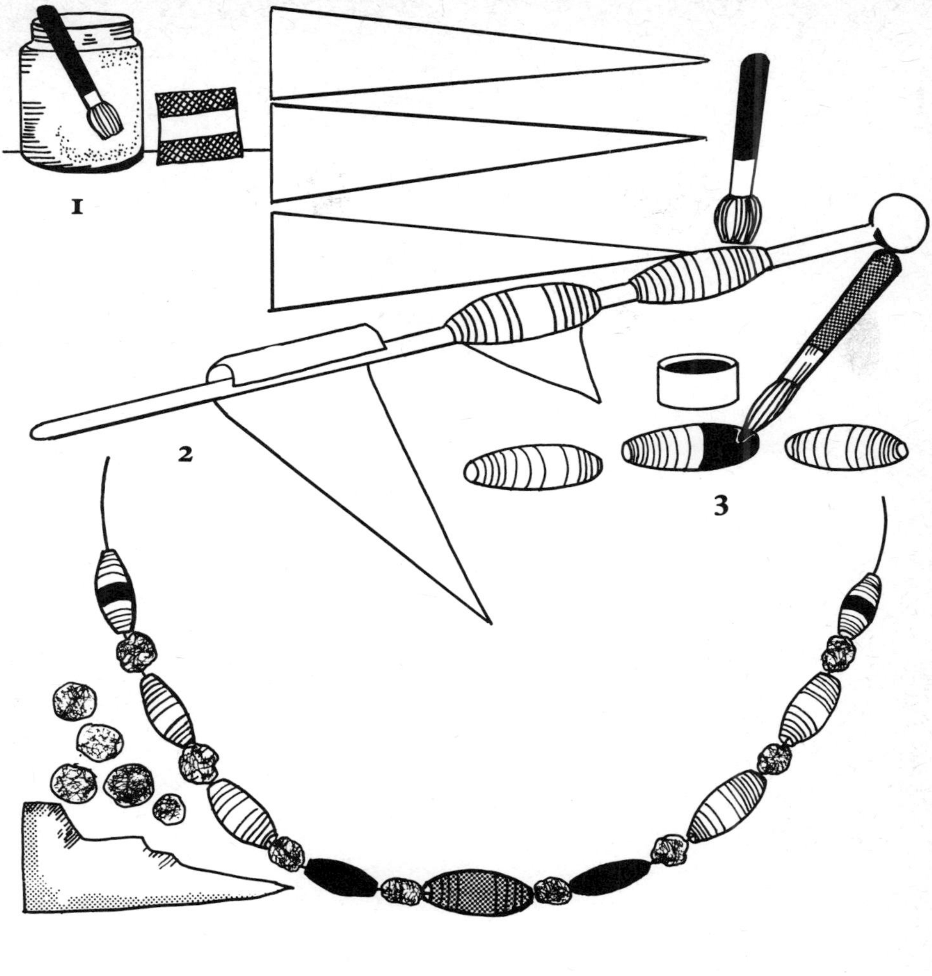

As you thread the beads you can put small crumpled up balls of tin foil in between to give them an extra sparkle.

If you decide to try making beads from home made flour clay or non-firing clay you can use the knitting needle again for making the holes. Push the beads onto it and leave them on it until they are dry.

Sun king

(See cover photograph)

The Inca indians of South America worshipped the sun. Their kings wore magnificent gold jewelry because it was thought their power came directly from the sun. They might have looked a little like this.

To make a sun king costume you need:
corrugated card
tin foil or silver wrapping paper
gold and silver paint and a brush
plain drinking straws
tabs from tin cans
two paper plates
old hair rollers
shirring elastic
foil baking trays and treacle tin lids
scissors, strong glue, paper clips, pencil

1 Draw and cut a large circle from the corrugated card. This will become the collar piece. Cut a slit up one side to the middle and then cut out a 'neck-hole'.

2 Paint the card silver. Leave it to dry.

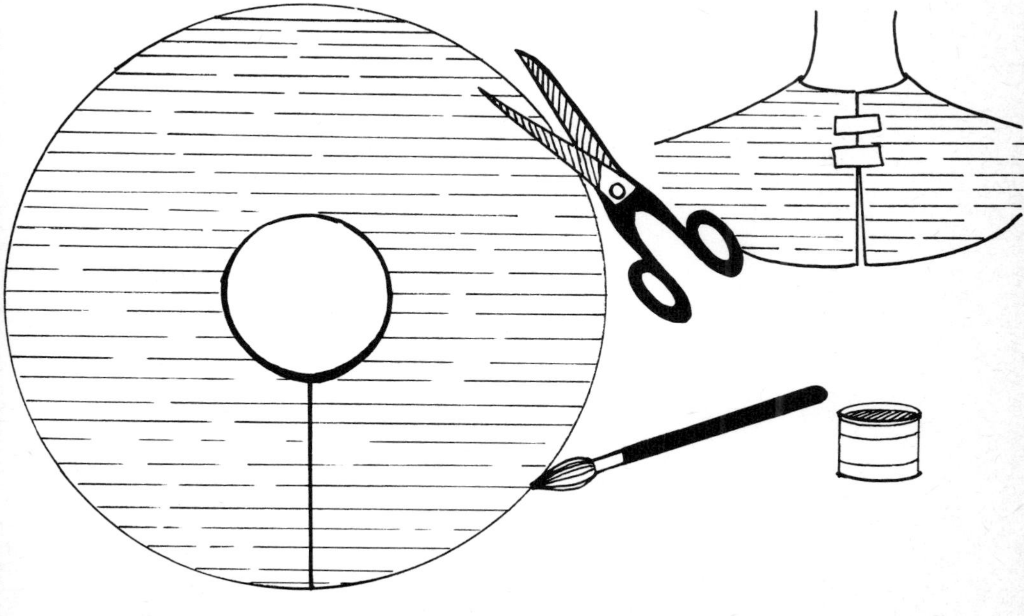

3 Paint the two paper plates and the drinking straws gold and leave them to dry. When they are ready, glue the straws round the edge of both plates to look like the sun's rays.

4 Attach a row of soft drink can tabs all along the edge of the collar piece by looping them onto paper clips and then pushing the clips through the card. Glue on some tin lids or shapes cut from foil baking trays.

5 Stick one of the suns to the front of the collar piece.

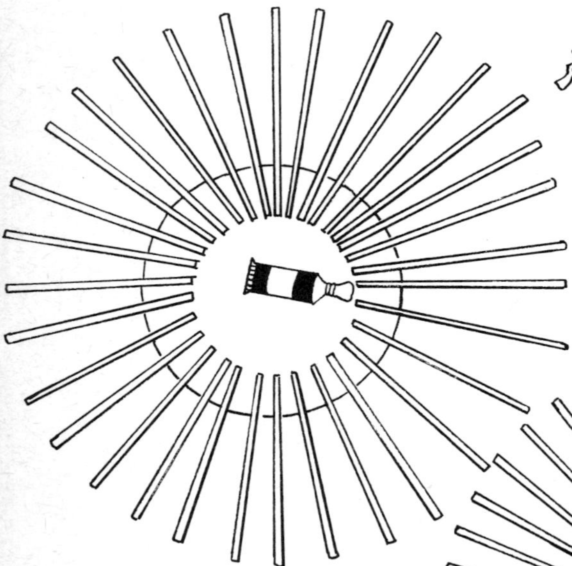

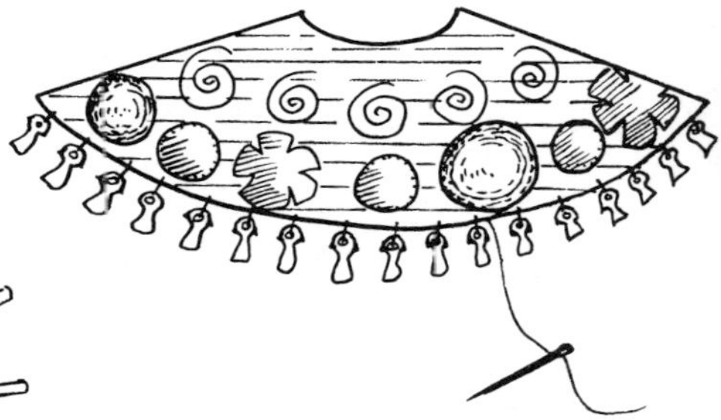

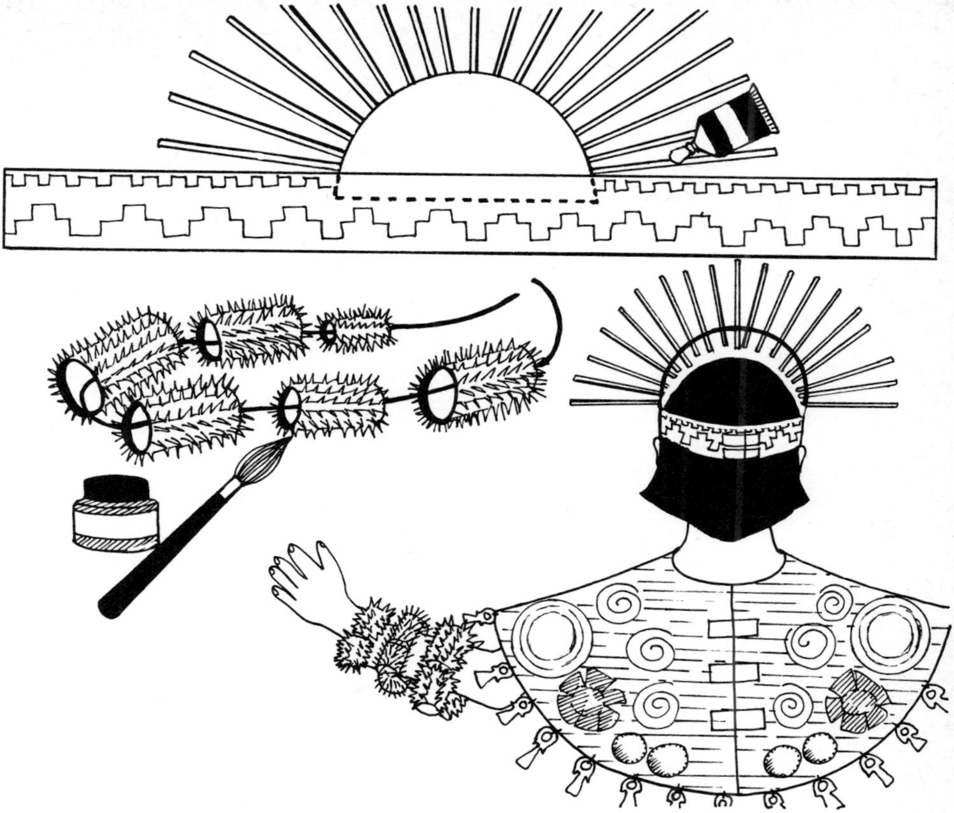

6 Cut out a band of card long enough to go round your head. Cover it with silver paper and tin foil. Cut the second sun in half. Glue it to the middle of the band and leave it to dry.

7 Paint some old hair rollers and thread them together with elastic to make two or three fierce looking arm bangles.

Put the collar on, followed by the crown. Join the ends together with Sellotape.

Arab head-dress

You need:
a piece of old material (about the size of a small towel)
curtain rings and needle and thread
assorted keys (including sardine keys)
milk – and ordinary bottle tops
coins, washers, card, Sellotape
glue (PVA), silver or gold paint

1 Cut a strip of card about as wide as the coins and long enough to fit round your head. Paint one side of the card silver or gold (or cover it with tin foil) and leave it to dry.

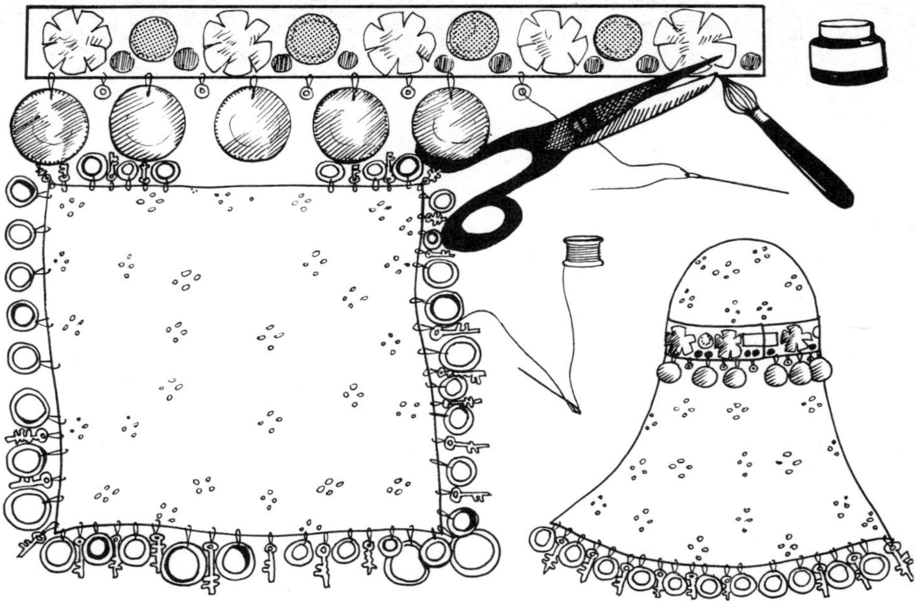

2 Sew the curtain rings and the keys round the four edges of the material. Leave a gap for your face in the middle of one side.

3 Attach the milk bottle tops and washers to the bottom edge of the card with the needle and thread. Glue on some coins and bottle tops and leave them to dry.

4 Place the material over your head so that the side without jewels is at the front. Wrap the cardboard crown round your head and then Sellotape the ends together so that it fits well.

Some Arabs living in desert tribes wear jewelry to show how wealthy they are. So the more coins and other metal trinkets you add to yours, the better.

Index